101
TINY CHANGES
TO BRIGHTEN YOUR DAY

101
TINY CHANGES
TO BRIGHTEN YOUR DAY

AILBHE MALONE

ILLUSTRATED BY NAOISE DOLAN

ICON

Published in the UK in 2018
and the USA in 2019
by Icon Books Ltd,
Omnibus Business Centre,
39–41 North Road,
London N7 9DP
email: info@iconbooks.com
www.iconbooks.com

Sold in the UK, Europe and Asia
by Faber & Faber Ltd,
Bloomsbury House,
74–77 Great Russell Street,
London WC1B 3DA or their agents

Distributed in the UK,
Europe and Asia
by Grantham Book Services,
Trent Road, Grantham NG31 7XQ

Distributed in the USA
by Publishers Group West,
1700 Fourth Street,
Berkeley, CA 94710

Distributed in Australia
and New Zealand
by Allen & Unwin Pty Ltd,
PO Box 8500,
83 Alexander Street,
Crows Nest, NSW 2065

Distributed in South Africa
by Jonathan Ball,
Office B4, The District,
41 Sir Lowry Road,
Woodstock 7925

Distributed in India
by Penguin Books India,
7th Floor, Infinity Tower – C,
DLF Cyber City,
Gurgaon 122002, Haryana

Distributed in Canada
by Publishers Group Canada,
76 Stafford Street, Unit 300
Toronto, Ontario M6J 2S1

ISBN: 978-178578-394-4

Text copyright © 2018 Ailbhe Malone

Illustrations copyright © 2018 Naoise Dolan

The author and artist have asserted their moral rights.

Typeset in Parango OT by Marie Doherty

Printed and bound in Great Britain
by Clays Ltd, Elcograf S.p.A.

CONTENTS

ABOUT THE AUTHOR

Ailbhe Malone is Lifestyle Editor at *BuzzFeed* UK and a founding member of the UK team. Her weekly self-care column for *BuzzFeed* ran from 2016–17. She consults on Lifestyle for *BuzzFeed* internationally and has featured as an industry expert on BBC's *The Apprentice*, and for Phaidon's *Where to Eat Pizza* (2016). Prior to *BuzzFeed*, she worked for *Nylon* (US), the *Guardian* (UK), *Heat* and *Wired*.

INTRODUCTION

Hello!

As you will see throughout this book – which I hope you are reading after purchasing, and not just skimming at the bookshop till (in which case: **Hiya! Please buy this. It's good, I promise.**) – I'm a big believer that small changes can have a big impact on your mood and well-being. And, although this book is about *you*, I thought I'd take a moment to talk about *me*. I mean, we're going on this journey together, so I might as well open up a bit.

For a long time, I thought my anxieties were par for the course. Who doesn't make a back-up plan in case their parents die and they have to provide for their siblings?

(Very few people do this.) Who doesn't panic if they don't arrive at the airport exactly two hours – three for long-haul flights – before their flight takes off? (Most people.) Who doesn't lull themselves to nervous sleep, revisiting all the mean jokes they once made in the pub to work acquaintances? (You can see where I'm going with this.)

My life went on in this tiring, anxious way for the better part of 28 years, until I started treatment for a generalised anxiety disorder. When I finally began treatment, I found the process of getting better overwhelming. For so long I had put myself at the bottom of the priority list, and it was all too much to try to climb my way back to the top. It was so important to me to worry about everybody else that I found it really difficult to believe that I was worth looking after.

I decided to begin looking after myself by focusing on the little things. I still found it difficult to say what I really wanted in certain situations, but I could test myself by deciding what I wanted on a smaller scale. Did I want to go to the gym after work, even though I was exhausted? *You need to lose some weight*, my brain said. Or would I just go home and watch TV and relax? *That sounds nice*, my body suggested.

I began to take what I thought of as considered risks – relying on my gut instinct and listening to what my body and soul needed, rather than what my burnt-out brain thought it needed. When I say 'risks', that's exactly what they felt like: like every deviation from a routine was inviting disaster. Through baby steps, I learned that the sky wouldn't come falling down if I put myself first every now and then.

Small things, like making my bed in the morning or being brave enough to tweet about my mental health, gave me a sense of accomplishment and made me feel like I wasn't alone. These steps, combined with medication and support from my therapist, helped me to open up and, like tarnish fading from silver, I began to shine again.

I began to treat myself more gently and more thoughtfully: I carried my self-esteem the way a dog carries a stick it's especially proud of. I trusted myself to believe that I was worth taking care of – and to see myself not as a project to be completed, but as a person trying to live their life. That's what I hope you'll get from this book.

In this book, I've gathered tips that will help rebalance your anxious mind – for when your self-esteem is low, and you don't believe you're worth looking after.

CARRY YOUR
SELF-ESTEEM THE
WAY A DOG CARRIES
A STICK IT'S
ESPECIALLY
PROUD OF

Maybe your confidence has been shaken by an unexpected twist at work, or perhaps you're finding a change in your personal life hard to deal with. **The point of this book isn't to solve your problems, but to help you learn to cut yourself a bit of slack.** There are practical tips to help you shine again, when you're not feeling the best, and they come in all sizes – from five-minute turnarounds to total attitude readjustments. This book is small enough to put in your backpack, or store by your bedside table – think of it as a guidebook for when you don't believe you're worth looking after.

At this point, I want to talk a bit about the commodification of self-care. It's something I feel conflicted about. I mean, hi, I got paid to write a book about it, which you, dear reader, have spent money on. On the one hand, if you want to spend money on making yourself feel better, then of course, do that. But on the other hand, someone is profiting from you trying to buy your way out of feeling bad about yourself. However, at the base of all this is the feeling that maybe you're not even worth spending money on.

I certainly struggle with this – if I buy myself something nice, I feel like I have to prove (to myself and others) that I have earned it. If someone compliments my new earrings, I'm quick to add that they were on sale – worried that someone will think that I'm too big for my boots. I'm aware enough of my privilege to understand that dithering over what buying a pair of nice earrings means for my self-esteem isn't an earth-shattering dilemma. But it can often feel like a big personal struggle, and it may do for you too. So, not for the last time, let me say: **you are worth spending time and money on.**

Unless you live in a yurt on a self-sustaining farm, spending money is part of your everyday life. But I recognise that you may have different means, so please take any tips about spending money with a pinch of salt, and a dose of whatever reality is appropriate for you.

With that spirit in mind, as you read the book, take pictures of your favourite tips, or grab a pen and make notes on those tips that don't work for you. These tiny changes are meant to brighten your day – if they don't, then leave them out!

TEENY TINY

The tips in this section focus on
the smallest mental adjustments.

Sometimes the idea of changing your habits is so overwhelming. It's hard to know where to start when you don't even know what you need. This means it can be infuriating when one is bombarded with wellness tips from all angles. (I am not unaware of the irony of writing this in a ~wellness tips~ book.) When well-meaning friends suggest yoga or yoghurts or whatever as a panacea, their good intentions can be almost heartbreaking. You might feel pushed and pulled between sceptically querying their suggestions, and desperately hoping that they'll work. *Don't you think I've tried yoga? Don't you think that if, bloody hell, there was a slight chance that yoga might actually work, I would be on that mat 24/7, while chowing down on some probiotic cherry yoghurt?*

For me, finding the right self-care regimen feels like playing one of those coin drop machines at the arcade – you know, the ones where you slowly drop in pennies as it pushes them over a ledge? Even though the game is tricky and requires constant input from me, there's also a chance that someday, I'll win. Incidentally, I do love this game and play it all the time (which probably tells you all you need to know about me).

In the same way that playing a coin drop machine won't win you enough money for a house deposit, these small mental adjustments won't change your life overnight. But they might distract you for a moment, or help you figure out what does and doesn't work, for *you*.

1

**Find an instant distraction
that you can turn to when
you're feeling worried.**

It could be as simple as thinking of
how you would cross a room without
touching the ground, or listing animals
alphabetically – anything that will focus
your tired brain on something different.

2

Try to find some internal stillness.

———

I know, I know, this is the meditation bit.
You could try a guided meditation app,
or you could lean into your daydreamer
tendencies. Create a scenario in which you
get to imagine rich detail; for example, I
can happily plan my dream lavish wedding,
or what I'd do if I were a pop star. Or, if you
don't have the time or desire to wander too
deep into daydreams, focus on something
concrete – like the buds on the plants on your
windowsill; marvel at how the sun's energy
is turning them into flowers ever so slowly.

3

If you have bad habits you're trying to change, like picking at your skin, or biting your nails, try replacing the sensation with something else. For instance, you might try holding an ice cube. (I tried this, and while the actual ice cube didn't work for me, the act of interrupting the impulse to pick did. I've also used a fidget spinner or a fidget cube too.)

4

Print out and frame some photos of family and friends.

You can buy frames really cheaply at stores like Tiger or Poundland, and there are quite a few online stores that let you print from Instagram for pennies. Having visual reminders of the people who love and care about you is like an arts and crafts comfort blanket.

5

Find a pause button in your day.
Instead of trying to push through
to the end of the working day,
make time to recharge.
And realise that 'recharging'
looks different for everyone
– maybe you like to chat to a
friend, or listen to a podcast
while taking a stroll around
the block. For example, I like
to stop around 3pm (schedule
permitting) and do the
crossword for fifteen minutes.

6

Say 'no' rather than yes. If plans and commitments are overwhelming you, it's ok to cancel or adjust them. If you're someone whose default is to make no plans, then make a couple of small, low-risk plans – maybe to walk around your local park with a friend, or to read two chapters of your book in a new coffee shop.

7

Spend some time making your bedroom as calm as possible.

———

This doesn't have to mean diffusers and whatnot – it can be smoothing down your sheets, plumping your pillows. You can make a really good and cheap pillow spray for pennies by mixing lavender essential oil, alcohol and water in an old, clean spray bottle.

8

Throw out clothes that make you feel bad.

———

BuzzFeed editor Arianna Rebolini wrote about throwing out clothes she had bought when her weight fluctuated due to an eating disorder:

I was beginning every single day with a terrible task – facing a closet that told me my body wasn't right, and choosing which way I'd like to be made physically uncomfortable that day. My clothes were undoing years of work toward accepting my body as-is, coaxing me into old beliefs.[1]

Are you holding on to clothes that don't reflect who you are anymore – or who you want to be? **Clothes are not an indicator of your worth** – if jeans don't fit, give them to a charity shop, and buy ones that make you feel good about your body.

9

Watch a TV show that reinforces how you feel.

This could be *Crazy Ex-Girlfriend*'s depiction of borderline personality disorder, *Unbreakable Kimmy Schmidt*'s determination to live alongside her PTSD, or even *RuPaul's Drag Race*, which endlessly preaches: 'If you can't love yourself, how the hell you gonna love somebody else?' All these shows are available on Netflix at the moment, btw – you can download and watch them whenever you want.

10

Upgrade your shower experience. Buy a shower gel that you love, or light a candle before you hop in. Spend an extra minute under the hottest water you can stand, and use a fresh, fluffy towel.

———

For a long time, I hated baths (so boring!) until I was given a waterproof Bluetooth speaker for Christmas. Now I listen to an audiobook while I wallow.

11

Write down one thing that you're looking forward to tomorrow.

—————

It can be literally anything – like eating fish finger sandwiches for lunch, or spotting a puppy in the park on the way in to work. Whatever makes you feel a small twitch of happiness.

12

Listen to an audiobook
from your childhood.

———

I've been working my way
through the *Harry Potter*
audiobooks, and each minute
feels like I'm cosily sat in the
backseat of my family car,
with my brother falling slowly
asleep on my shoulder.

13

Invest in one thing that makes your day a little brighter.

Whether that's a specific type of pen you like, or a water bottle in a bright colour. Just something that makes you smile when you look at it. My desk at work is surrounded with dumb trinkets, and I'm like a magpie in stationery shops: I pick up pens and highlighters that feel pleasing to me.

TAKE A WALK ON
THE WILD SIDE

The tips in this section focus on
the outdoors, and connecting
with the real world.

The 'real world' doesn't have to mean leafy parks – it can be a local café, or the home of a friend who lives around the corner from you. So much emphasis is placed on flowers and nature and whatnot – and, although that's great, you may not have access to a personal green space; it's a huge luxury. It took me a long time to get access to a 'proper garden', but I found great peace in noodling with supermarket potted herbs, and tending to cacti on the windowsill.

What I'm saying is, it's all relative. The best way to approach this chapter is to think about the sensation you get from interacting with new stimuli. If you're someone who's outdoorsy, let's take that literally. If you're not – or if you're not feeling great – take things easier. The sensation of looking at the scenery while eating your sandwiches on a mountain hike might not be analogous to watching the leaves on a fern by your sink slowly unfurl, but they're both jaw-dropping examples of nature carrying on, even when everything else is a shambles.

Outside can mean different things for different people. This chapter is all about finding an external stimulus that works for you – so **try not to compare your buds to someone else's blooms**. The same way someone's tiny studio flat can look curated and chic on Instagram while being a nightmare to live in, so can their garden. You may see hashtags like #monsteramonday and think, *I'll never be an Instagram gardener, with my wilty basil and weirdly hardy geranium* – but you will never know how many monsteras that 'grammer has killed in advance of the shot.

WOW, NATURE IS LOVELY EVEN WITH #NOFILTER
(BUT A SLIGHT PURPLE TINT NEVER HURTS)

14

If you're feeling overwhelmed and caught up in your head, try to focus on textures.

Remember that scene in *Amélie* where she plunges her hand into a bag of grain? Stroke the fabric of the chair you're sitting on, and concentrate on how it feels against your fingertips. Or run your hands under a cold tap, feeling the water slide down your fingers. Take a deep breath in – and out – then bring your mind back to the present.

15

Take half an hour and get to know your area. Stomp through the grass in the park, and inspect the flowers that grow there. Is your local park a bit shabby? What are the trees like? Are they young or old? Fill your imagination with the possibilities of the park, and take joy in knowing that every time you visit, it will have changed.

16

Add a walk to your day.

———

This could mean incorporating it
into your commute – e.g. get off
a stop earlier or later. Or it could
mean getting together with some
other people to move around.
In Bryony Gordon's great book
Mad Girl, she talks about how she
discovered moving helped her OCD:

> *All I am doing for that twenty minutes or*
> *so is trying to stay alive. The only thing*
> *that matters is that I continue to breathe ...*
> *after a jog, everything feels a smidgeon*
> *more bearable than it did before a jog.*[2]

17

Take note of the people
you see every day on
your walk to work.

If I'm feeling low and obsessing
over some intrusive thoughts,
it's a great balm to me to
know that Charlie the dog
will be running for a stick in
the park at about 9.10am.

18

Experience nature through your phone.

Take a photo of a green space that you love – it can be something from a holiday, or even a snap of supermarket flowers that add a dash of colour. What's really cool is that you don't actually have to *be* in nature to reap the benefits of the outdoors. There are loads of studies which show that even looking at photos of 'restorative environments' (like a mountain range!) has a positive impact on 'mental fatigue'. Good reason to change your desktop to a chill nature pic.[3]

19

Buy a little plant.

If the idea of going to a garden centre to stock up on compost and start a big project fills you with dread, buy a little succulent (they don't need any attention and cost £2 or so). Plus, most supermarkets have a house plant section, so you can pick one up while doing your food shop. If you work in an office, or a regular work space, bring that plant in. A 2010 study by researchers at Sydney University showed that even one plant is enough to reduce 'stress and negative mood states' over a three-month period.[4]

20

Read in a new location. You could sit under a shady tree *Brideshead Revisited*-style, but if that gives you a crick in your neck, then why not try sitting on a park bench? And who says it has to be a book, rather than a podcast? Find what works for you.

21

Start gardening on a small scale. Gardening on a large scale is expensive, but you'd be amazed by how many things you can grow on a windowsill, and you'd be even more amazed by how easy it is. If you don't have the space to store compost, etc., then buying some fresh supermarket herbs is a great way to start. Alice Vincent's *How to Grow Stuff* (in the Reading List) will give you all the tips you need.

22

Not into actual gardening? Why not garden by proxy – visit a park or local garden and think about which plants you'd keep and which you'd replace.

23

Try to feel a connection to the food you eat.

———

Eat an apple and think about where it came from – all the care that has gone into making sure you get to eat the juiciest one. Imagine the seeds growing in the ground, and the hands picking the fruit. Ruby Tandoh (who you might remember from *The Great British Bake Off*) is the absolute queen of thinking about eating in a positive and fulfilling way. Recently, she tweeted her favourite food moments, which included:

putting a candle in fondant icing, the sweet dregs of cereal milk, the inevitable bit of melty cheese stuck to the wrapper of yr cheeseburger, pie gravy making the underside of the pastry all soggy, butter dripping thru the lil crumpet holes.[5]

MAKING YOUR PHONE WORK FOR YOU

The tips in this section focus on
making your phone a tool for good,
and how to get the most out of your
phone, without it ruling your life.

Most of us have complicated relationships with our phones, myself included. On the one hand, my whole life is there. Scrolling through my photos reveals years of memories: I can see my mum before she was sick with cancer, during her treatment, and getting better. Flicking over to WhatsApp, I can dive into my friendship group's five-year-long group chat. And searching Google Maps for houses where I have once lived is like tracing an old explorer's map of my twenties.

On the other hand, my phone overwhelms me. Apps like Instagram feel like a conveyor belt of reasons why I'm failing, as I lie in bed and flick through everybody else's successes. Meanwhile, Twitter's incessant notifications make me feel on edge, and Facebook makes me feel guilty about not staying in touch with old friends.

I panic when my phone runs out of battery (*What if I miss an important call?*), but I hate myself for draining the battery because I have been refreshing rolling bad news. Sound familiar?

This is no way to live. Approaching our phones like this is setting ourselves up for disaster. A phone is just a tool – like a hammer, it can help destroy things, or it can help build them. So, here are some ways to make your phone a creative tool.

MIRROR MIRROR ON THE WALL, WHO'S THE **SHAREDEST** OF THEM ALL?

24

Change your background to a photo that makes you smile.

It could be your pet – or a celebrity animal (I'm not judging). It could be your best friend. Or it could just be a photo of somewhere you'd like to visit.

25

Change your alarm to a noise that you don't dread.

Maybe it's your favourite song or a sound that reminds you of a holiday, or maybe it's an old-school telephone noise. Remember, you're going to hear it every morning, so you may as well like it.

26

Use the 'Notes' app on your phone to write down things that you're proud of. The next time you're being hard on yourself, flip open the app and glance down at the best things about yourself. These don't have to be full statements; they can be as simple as 'left work right on time' or something you like about yourself.

27

Make a playlist of all
your favourite songs,
so that you can listen to
them when you need to.

28

Download a white
noise app.

———

Or search YouTube for
'white noise'. The sound is not
obtrusive, and it might help to
drown out circling thoughts or
background noises. I like to have
it on in my headphones when
I'm working on a tricky task.

29

Turn off notifications on your phone.

There is no such thing as an urgent Facebook message. There's an interesting study by the Future Work Centre about phone messages. They call push notifications a 'toxic source of stress', explaining that the combination of an emotional learned response to messages and an 'unwritten organisational etiquette around email' doubles down into a no-win situation.[6] All of which is to say: push back against answering everything straight away.

If it's urgent, they'll call you.

30

Download a new podcast.

I love the 'Singing Bones'
podcast. It's a podcast
about the origins of fairy
tales, and I've learned so
much about fairy tales from
around the world, as well as
the critical theory behind
some of my favourite ones.

31

Leave your phone in another room, when you can, *especially* at night-time before you go to bed. Blue light from your phone affects your circadian rhythms (that's your sleep cycle). In a 2014 study comparing people who used an e-reader before bed to those who read printed books, Dr Anne-Marie Chang found that:

Participants who read on light-emitting devices took longer to fall asleep, had less REM sleep [the phase when we dream] and had higher alertness before bedtime [than those people who read printed books]. We also found that after an eight-hour sleep episode, those who read on the light-emitting device were sleepier and took longer to wake up.[7]

32

Try a sleep tracker if you're struggling with poor-quality sleep. It might help you to notice the effects of external factors. (Does red wine give you weird dreams? Do you sleep better after exercise?) If you don't want to be in thrall to a gadget, you could track your sleep in a journal, and notice if any external factors are adding up.

33

Don't look at your phone
for at least ten minutes
after you wake up.

———

Although I am pathetically tied to
my phone, I refuse to let it set the
agenda for my day. I try not to look
at Instagram immediately after
waking up. Instead, I try to stretch
and look at the sun coming through
the curtains. Easing into the day in a
more mindful way sets your mood to
being less anxious, from the outset.

34

Write down one good thing
that has happened to you
today, before you go to bed.

This could be a nice way to transition
from actively engaging with your
phone before you go to sleep. Think
of these notes as saying goodnight
to your screen – the last thing
you do on it before you check in
again in the morning. You could
write your good thing in the notes
section of your phone, if you like;
it's a great list to scroll through at
a time when you're feeling glum.

35

Gather photos that make you feel good. Make an inspiration board on Pinterest of all your achievements and every nice thing you believe about yourself. And when I say 'achievements', I mean memories or photos that make you feel good. It could be a screenshot of a nice email, or a photo of your group of friends – anything that helps visualise a positive moment.

36

Remove your work email app from your phone.

37

Make a folder with all
the apps that you'll need
when you have a bad
day. On those days, don't
look at anything else on
your phone; just head
straight for the folder.

38

Let the battery die,
and realise that it's not
the end of the world.

PREP FOR DARKER DAYS

The tips in this section focus on how to prepare yourself for days when you don't feel great, on days when you do.

There's no way around this. Some days, or weeks, you are going to feel like everything is too much. And I'm really sorry. There's nothing I can do about that either. I'm talking about those low points when the day-to-day is more than you can handle, and you're just blobbing along. The good news is that there are a handful of things you can do to prepare, as you'll see in this chapter.

If I'm honest, writing this chapter made me feel like a bit of a fraud. It's difficult to tell you, lovely reader, how to prep for darker days when I'm still figuring it out myself. I know that (as usual) I'm being too hard on myself. If I look back to when I first started treatment for my anxiety and how I handled Bad Brain Days, and compare that to now, I can see a world of difference. I'm far more aware of my triggers and the warning signs, and I've got some small changes that I can make to help myself feel better. And I think that's the most important bit to recognise – that you might not have it all 'figured out' or get to a point of being 100 per cent well.

Don't think of this chapter as a nuclear bunker that will shield you from all harm. Nothing can do that. Instead, you could use it as a talisman or a comfort blanket. Each time you turn to it you might learn something new that can help you on your journey.

So, it's pen and paper time: you could take inspiration from the chapters you've read so far, and mix in tips from this chapter, to create some practical changes that will mean your brain can autopilot for a bit, until you feel better again. But if that feeling of being overwhelmed doesn't ease, talk to your friends, your family, your doctor. And remember there are hotlines that you can call at any time.

39

On a day when you have plenty of energy, batch cook a couple of healthy meals and put them in your freezer.

I love making a big batch of minestrone, and it reheats really well. If your freezer isn't big enough, then you could buy loads of tins of soup – or packet noodles. It doesn't really matter what you store, just make sure it's something that you can cook easily. Similarly, why not prepare a batch of cookie dough and freeze small handfuls of dough in a tub or sandwich bag; you can pop a few balls straight onto a baking tray and bake a fresh batch of cookies with minimum effort.

40

... But also LOL to minestrone and baking fresh cookies. Keep easy-to-cook comfort food, like oven chips and fish fingers, in your freezer at all times, and have some tinned food in the cupboard.

You're going to need to eat, and sometimes you just: a) won't want to cook; or b) can't fathom going to the shops to buy food that you could cook. Sometimes 'eating well' means eating whatever will make you feel good and whatever you can summon up the energy to cook. Plus things like tinned spaghetti hoops or baked beans won't kill you when eaten cold, and tinned peach slices are a fantastic way to get some vitamin C.

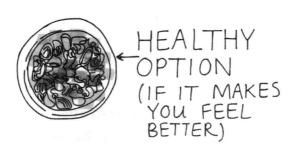

HEALTHY
OPTION
(IF IT MAKES
YOU FEEL
BETTER)

OVEN
LOVE-IN

ALSO A
HEALTHY OPTION
(IF IT MAKES YOU
FEEL BETTER)

(GO FIGURE)

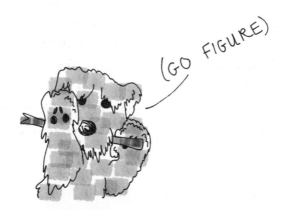

41

Keep a list on your phone of things that cheer you up – keep it in whichever notes app you regularly use. It could be a 'raindrops and roses'-type of list, or it could be screenshots of the nice texts and emails your friends have sent you.

42

Write an email to
yourself that you can
read when you're feeling
down. Write it as if
you were writing to a
dearly beloved friend.

43

Make a playlist of chart hits from your younger years.

When I'm not feeling well, new music is too overwhelming for me – I find it hard to concentrate and I get stressed out. So I like to listen to songs I know all the words to, but don't particularly love. At this point, Flo Rida singing about 'the boots with the furrrrrrr' is like white noise to me.

44

Buy DVDs of your old favourite movies. When your brain is whirring, you might find streaming sites like Netflix too stressful to navigate; at those times you can slot in a DVD and know that you don't need to make any more decisions for at least 90 minutes.

45

Ask a friend in advance to be your buddy – get them to agree to come by and check in on you if you're feeling low, and ask them not to let you cancel.

46

Buy some nice cosy clothes.

That doesn't have to mean cashmere joggers but maybe a pair of comfy H&M tracksuit bottoms. Make a conscious decision to be comfortable at home. For a lot of us, our 'cosy clothes' aren't actually that cosy; they're old t-shirts that have come to the end of their life. Decide to make your leisure-wear something you actually enjoy wearing, not an afterthought.

47

Have some inspirational materials to hand.

―――

Wait, come back! I'm not talking about italicised Pinterest quotes. I mean some quotes from people dealing with the same stuff as you, to help you remember that you're not alone. Whether it's Stephen Fry talking about his depression and bipolar disorder, or Rachel Bloom from *Crazy Ex-Girlfriend* talking about how important it was to showcase a successful character with borderline personality disorder. If the idea of relying on your phone makes you feel nervous, you could always order some books from the library and photocopy the passages you feel most strongly about.

48

Practise allowing yourself to feel however you're feeling.

It's exhausting to feel cross at yourself for feeling low, or to admonish yourself for having a panic attack. The hardest part is accepting the uncomfortable feelings, and facing them head on – believing that what you're feeling is real, and that you are worth being kind to.

49

Buy in some anti-bac wipes, and some face wipes. Cleaning a house is a huge effort if you're not well, but half-heartedly wiping down a surface with a Dettol wet wipe will make a world of difference.

ALL TOO MUCH

The tips in this section focus on small victories, for when you're feeling really down or exhausted.

It's all well and good making extravagant plans to look after yourself when you're feeling well. Who doesn't love a spa day? But the real challenge is taking care of yourself when you really and truly don't believe you're worth it. That's where Self-care 101 comes in.

When I was at my lowest, the idea of taking five minutes from my day to take care of myself was ludicrous. (It's incredible now, but there were two weeks when I genuinely thought THE CIA WERE TAPPING MY PHONE.) My frazzled brain was pinging from left to right to upside down; there was no *time* to focus on me. Even once I began to get better, I still found looking after myself on the bottom of the to-do list. But there were some stress relievers that I found useful, and when I got better, they still held up.

So let's not think about these tips as 'ways to fix a bad mood'. Instead, **let's call them 'pause buttons'**. Think about it in the same way as when you're playing Temple Run and you're barrelling towards a crash: you can't avoid the crash (and if you could, you wouldn't be playing Temple Run – crashing is an inevitable part of the game). Instead of crashing into the mask, you can press pause. The crash will be there, waiting for you, and you'll still have to restart the level after it happens, but at least you can take a moment to catch your breath.

Really think about how to adapt these tips so that they work for you. If, for instance, committing to plans instead of cancelling supports your mental health better, then do that and ignore Tip 50.

Once you've read this chapter, I'd encourage you to share it with your friends and loved ones – especially if you're going through a difficult period. When someone they love (that's *you*) isn't feeling well, it's terrifying and they can feel helpless. It might be useful for them to read these tips so that they know how they might be able to help.

VICTORY #1:
WINDOW SUCCESSFULLY OPENED

VICTORY #2:
BED SUCCESSFULLY MADE

VICTORY #3:
BED **VERY** SUCCESSFULLY LAIN IN

50

Give yourself permission to just cancel your plans. Your friends will understand. Your family will understand. You don't have to give an excuse, apart from 'I don't feel great'. Switch your phone to airplane mode, and just rest.

———

But tell somebody before you decide to switch your phone to airplane mode. It is absolutely terrifying not to be able to get in touch with someone you love when you know their mental health is at a low point – as an anxious person, I always assume the worst has happened.

51

Have a glass of water:
you need to stay hydrated.
And just taking the time
out to fetch and drink
a cool glass of water
is a soothing act in itself.
Keep a bottle of water
by your bedside, so that
it's automatically there
when you need it.

52

Take your meds.

———

I should thank everyone on
Tumblr who has repeated this
mantra (and the tip about
keeping hydrated) enough
that it is almost my default
mode in a stressful situation.

53

Make your bed. By this I mean pull the duvet cover up and straighten your pillows. This isn't the time for changing your sheets or plumping your pillows. If all you do today is make your bed, that's still an achievement. Even if you get right back in it again, the feeling of crisper sheets and smooth pillows will soothe you.

54

Tell someone you trust how you're feeling. This sounds like more than a 'tiny adjustment', I know, but you don't have to say everything if you don't want to. If all you can say is 'I'm feeling really stressed about this situation at work', that's cool. People love you and want to help you. I promise.

55

Give yourself time.

———

One of biggest demands of self-care is learning to accept that some things take time. If you're feeling awful and can't figure out left from right, it's really difficult to take a moment to reset. But what you can do is say: 'When I feel better, because *I will feel better*, I'm going to need some time to recover, and *I will take that time.*'

56

If you live in a cold climate, invest in a hot-water bottle.

———

When I'm low and sluggish, the idea of leaving my snuggly bed is not inviting. But a hot-water bottle costs £3, and filling it up is a valid reason to leave your bed and sit on the sofa for a bit.

57

Eat something.

Even if you've not got much appetite. It does not matter what you eat. Eat whatever makes you feel good. Eat toast, eat McDonald's, eat cereal. Now is not the time for mindful cooking or turmeric lattes; it's the time for basic nourishment and whatever will keep you going. If you're eating in bed, try to put the dishes in the sink afterwards.

58

Stretch.

You can find lots of videos on
YouTube for easy stretches –
including some you can do from
bed (search: 'safe stretches for
beginners'). Even if you're lying
down, brain whirring, you'll
likely feel a bit better if you
ease the crick in your neck.

59

Occupy your hands. If your brain is racing and you're unable to focus, try using a fidget spinner or something tactile like putty (there's a brand called Thinking Putty which, as well as being great to hold, is colour-changing). If you like colouring in, you could try this too.

I'VE ONLY GOT FIVE MINUTES

The tips in this section focus on time-saving and last-minute adjustments. Nothing too big – just little tweaks that might help lift your mood.

Without being too Eeyore about it, life is hard, and responsibilities are relentless. And sometimes there just isn't time to focus on yourself. That's not your fault; nor is it anyone else's. I am guilty of bumping myself to the bottom of my to-do list, promising frantically in my diary to set aside self-care time the next day, then the next day instead, then the next. When I'm feeling anxious, it's tempting to try to address the biggest issues first, and put off the smaller tasks until last. But let's think about this: drinking two litres of water tomorrow isn't the same as drinking a glass today. Consistency of self-care is better than volume.

Taking a five-minute pause to check in with yourself will save you a headache in the long run – both literally and figuratively.

Also, understand that **'five minutes' is a loose bracket of time** – please don't follow the timings too strictly.

60

Listen to your favourite
song, really bloody loud.
If you can get away
without headphones,
do it. Just blast it.

61

Watch a favourite film clip on YouTube.

I'm not saying you should spend 90 minutes watching *Hercules*, but a five-minute burst won't hurt.

62

Send a postcard to a
friend in your hometown.
You don't have to share
any huge news with them
– it's more of a check-in
than a missive. Tell them
what you plan to have
for lunch today – or the
names of the cats that
live on your street.

63

Download a meditation app. Even if you don't end up completing the programme, learning to connect with your breath is a useful way to ground yourself in stressful situations.

64

Pack your lunch the day before. Think about how delicious it will be, and feel compassion towards yourself for looking after your needs.

65

Clean one room in your house for five minutes.

———

One of the best quick fixes for when you feel your life is spiralling out of control is tidying something small. Wipe down the surfaces, or put away the clean clothes that have piled up in your bedroom.

66

Make the perfect cup of tea. Add a biscuit, if you like.

67

Block out a piece of time in your calendar for yourself. Take a critical look at your week, and figure out which day is your most stressful. Then keep aside one hour on that day to let yourself catch up.

(It's OK to reschedule. I used to take pride in the fact that I kept to a tight schedule. If I said we would meet at 10.15, I would be there at 10.11! But living like that is exhausting, and puts others' needs ahead of your own.)

68

Spend your money in a way that makes you feel good.

Donate to charity if you can, or drop off some food at your local food bank when you do your big grocery shop. If accessibility is an issue, some initiatives, like Beauty Banks, let you shop online for the supplies charities need.[8]

69

If you don't have money to
spare, that's OK! You might
have time to spare, which you
could use in a way that will
make you feel good. Volunteer
at a local charity shop one
day a month, or get involved
with an afternoon club in your
area. You could even call your
local library and see if they're
accepting book donations.

70

Give a sincere compliment. Tell somebody what you admire about them.

If this is awkward to do in real life ('Oh, hello, Adam. I admire your sense of decorum!'), then you could always text it. Sometimes it's hard to think of things you like about yourself, but you can always find something you like about someone else. In doing so, think about why you admire that quality – and what it says about you.

71

Catch your breath. Take
a moment. Deep breath
in. Deep breath out.

72

Imagine your dream party, in detail.

———

This is one of my favourite
daydreams – who will
I invite? What will I serve?
Will there be a dress code?

73

Write down one good
thing that has happened
to you today. Big or small.

74

Have a bathroom disco.
Find a cubicle, lock
the door, and have a
mini *Footloose* party.

DEALING WITH THE INTERNET (BECAUSE SOMETIMES IT IS JUST THE **WORST**)

The tips in this section focus on looking after your mental health while on the internet.

Most of us have lived a large part of our lives online. We meet our partners online (I met mine on Myspace, back in the days when having coded your own HTML background earned serious kudos). Our careers may focus on, or rely on using, the internet, and our leisure time is also interlinked with the internet. But it is so draining. With one quick search term, I can access everything I need in order to feel bad about myself. *Hating how I look?* There's Instagram. *Hating my job?* There's LinkedIn. *Hating my low self-esteem?* There's YouTube. And no matter how many people tell you to harness these outlets for good (I mean, that *is* essentially the theme of this chapter), it's so alluring to go to those corners of the internet which validate every bad thought you've ever had about yourself. It's like the Mirror of Erised in *Harry Potter*, except, instead of showing you your heart's desire, it shows you the dark and mouldy corners of your midnight monkey-brain.

The worst bit about the internet though, is how it gives everyone a voice. Even my granny (for whom I once had to print out a blog post to show her, because she didn't understand what a blog post was) knows to say: **'Don't read the comments.'** But they lure you in. For every lovely comment on how a piece of mine has helped someone, there are three that say: 'Who wrote this, a work experience student?' or 'Sort out your eyebrows, love.' The general criticisms I can shake off, but the researched ones really hurt. I carry them with me and nurture them – my brain worrying them like a wound.

But it doesn't have to be like this! I often think of what it would have been like to be a caveman, and how incredible the idea of fire would have been. What is this magical business that makes Ugg's life easier? (I know, I know, my caveman name is Ugg.) But at the same time, it burns! This is kind of how I feel about the internet. It can make our lives so much easier, and it can illuminate connections with people all across the world, such that we can instantly connect with and be understood by others – but it can also really hurt us. So let's approach it like a flame and make it work for us – while knowing that, just like a flickering match, we can extinguish it whenever we want.

75

Approach the internet like a mum.

The greatest decision I ever made was to stop trying to be cool online. I tag friends in things on Facebook (like a mum!). I leave comments on celebrities' Instagrams (like a mum!). I join in on Twitter conversations (like a mum!). Once I stopped trying to ~curate my brand~ online, I was able to reassess what I really wanted from social networks: a space to share with and connect to my friends.

76

If a comment gets to you, try to think why. Read it in the voice of someone close to you – is it a genuine query they'd raise? Or is it something cruel they'd never say? It's normal to have your feelings hurt by a mean comment online! But there is no need to pin it to your breast like a mourning brooch.

77

Use Pinterest as an achievements noticeboard.

Aspirational social networks are intense, but you can use them exactly how you want. If you want to create an imaginary wedding board, or a scrapbook of your best tweets or your cutest Facebook pics, do it. You don't have to restrict it to things that can be easily visualised – if you've had a success at your job, why not make an image to represent that?

78

Set times to be online
and times to be offline.
You could delete the
Twitter or Facebook
app from your phone,
or set a resolution only
to check them between
9–5 Monday–Friday.

79

Find a part of the internet
that makes you feel good.

———

I love Calming Manatee,
which is exactly what
it sounds like: a site
that generates photos
of chill sea cows.

80

Unfollow the person you hate on Twitter. Just stop hate-reading!

81

Organise your inbox if it makes you feel in control; ignore the idea of inbox zero if it stresses you out.

82

Install an app like
SelfControl (or Cold
Turkey if you're on a
PC) to stop yourself
obsessively looking up
stuff – it's a free program
that blocks access to
certain websites for a
set amount of time.

83

Join a closed Facebook group where you can explore your feelings in a safe space. They can be a great place to meet people who are having the same issues as you, without the facelessness of forums or the transience of other online communities. Search for groups that appeal to you, like 'Women with Anxiety'. You might have to request permission from the moderator to join, but don't worry – they're generally great, supportive spaces.

84

Find a YouTube channel that calls to you.

———

I can't get enough of Yoga with Adriene – free, chill, inclusive yoga classes with an instructor who stops every few minutes to make sure you're doing what feels best for you. In an ecosystem of crunches and HIIT, it's so great to have a pocket of positivity. She's also got the best dog, if that floats your boat.

85

Reflect on how far you've come by browsing your own Instagram feed.

I like to scroll back through Instagram and remember how I was feeling behind the scenes of the photos. *Yeah, I look cute,* I might think, *but I was having a panic attack at that party.* Even if I'm not feeling great in the present moment, it's helpful to remember that there have been similar times in the past and that I've got through them.

LETTING OTHERS HELP YOU
(YOU'RE NOT ALONE!)

The tips in this section focus on letting your friends and family know how to help you.

Man, it is hard to be a person in this world.
But, as universal a concept as that is, it's
a very hard one to articulate to friends
and family. And it's all the more difficult
to articulate after 'the worst is over': the
hardest part isn't telling people how you're
feeling (there's a certain bombast to that
speech), it's telling them, six months later,
that you're still not 'fixed', but you're
working on it.

When I was twenty, I worked as a
chambermaid in a fancy hotel. There were
about 30 of us on shift, each with our list
of rooms to clean. I was ten minutes away
from finishing my shift and had one room
left to clean. And it was a total bombsite
– the parents had booked their six year old
into an adjoining suite, and she'd trashed
the place. I'm talking lipstick on the walls,
toilet paper everywhere, total carnage.

I didn't know what to do. I was totally out of my depth. I called another maid on the staff phone and asked for a hand. She came in, took a look at the room and paged everyone else who was about to finish their shift. Like the animals who swoop in to help Cinderella, my colleagues helped me clean the room and get out in time. The takeaway is this: **you've got to let people help you, even if you feel like you've got it covered.** (Spoiler alert: you generally do not have it covered.)

In a roundabout way, that's what living with an ongoing mental illness feels like. The horror of showing vulnerability, or the challenge of even beginning to talk about how you're feeling, means that getting better after mental illness can be really lonely. Though it may not feel like it at the time, there are so many resources available to help you begin to talk about how you're feeling.[9] But the follow-up – or even the realisation that you may be dealing with a chronic ongoing condition – is challenging.

So, let people in, and trust them. Perhaps your mum doesn't know what a panic attack feels like – but she wants to. Your friends and family are radiating love and warmth; like a sunflower, turn your face towards it.

SUN
(= LOVE/SUPPORT
OF FRIENDS & FAM)

SUNFLOWER
(=YOU)

86

Tell your friends and family what being well looks like for you.

The mental health charity Mind has a really useful tool called the Wellness Action Plan.[10] It helps plot out any triggers, warning signs, treatments, and what helps keep you well. Tell those close to you what helps and what doesn't.

87

Use films and TV to open a difficult conversation.

If you don't know where to start, here's an example: while watching *New Girl* with my boyfriend, he mentioned that he often feels like Jess does. Her boyfriend Nick is funny, handsome and always down on himself. It makes Jess really upset. My boyfriend said, 'That's how I feel when you talk yourself down.' Using characters as a proxy can make it easier to gain some perspective.

88

If you're having
a difficult time, say so.

For example, I used to doggedly stay
at events and have silent anxiety
attacks – smiling and chatting, while
thinking about how everybody in the
room loathed me – before making
my excuses and leaving. But now I
trust my friends enough to say, 'I'm
feeling a bit overwhelmed; I think
I'm going to take a walk.' Try not to
put 'being polite' ahead of your own
well-being. It's better to speak up.

89

Create analogies or refer to experiences that mirror your own to help people understand what you're feeling. Nobody is a mind reader. I like to say that when I'm anxious, my brain feels like a washing machine going around.

In her great book, *Cheer Up Love*, comedian Susan Calman describes her depression as a 'crab of hate'. She writes:

You might think it's a slightly foolish endeavour to create a character around your own particular feelings, but give it a go. It can help create shorthand for reference that, as with my wife, can make things easier to explain to people.[11]

90

List your responsibilities and see how many actually matter. You can then talk through how each makes you feel with your friends and family.

91

Give your friends and family the language with which to speak to you, and try to learn their personal languages too.

———

Author Gary Chapman posits that people show their love in different ways – such as with words of affirmation, giving gifts, or spending quality time together.[12] If your way of showing love is spending quality time with someone, then you may get frustrated when they prefer to text their support. Try to figure out how you like people to support you, and let them know.

92

Ask a friend to record something
on their phone that you can
listen to when you're low.

When I was small, my mum recorded
herself reading our bedtime stories,
and, although I no longer have a
way to play the cassette tape, I still
think of it when I'm worried, and her
voice telling me how the Lambton
Worm was found down a well.

BIG AND BRAVE

The tips in this section focus
on large changes, or things
that require more effort.

Dear friends, you've made it to the end. At this point, I really hope you understand the central point of this book – that 'self-care' is focused on the self because it's all down to you, and what feels good to you. It's also about recognising that some things that *feel* good to you, aren't actually good for you anymore. I'm not just talking about drinking alcohol, or exercising too much, or all those things that you're supposed to New-Year-New-You away. I'm also talking about habits that feel like a security blanket, but which aren't actually comforting you – like arriving to the airport early, but fixating on not missing your flight so much that you don't take any pleasure from knowing you're on time, exploring the departure lounge, or getting to look forward to your trip.

If your comfort-blanket habits aren't actually comforting you, then it's time for Big and Brave changes to ditch your problem habits and replace them with healthier ones. Alongside these changes, I would strongly recommend that you talk to someone and get professional help. Some changes are too big to make solo. Having a licensed professional there to guide you is wise. Therapy will help you understand the roots of your habits and how to change them in a controlled and safe way.

I cannot tell you how helpful ongoing therapy has been for me personally – while taking anti-anxiety medication helped calm the voices in my head (I like to describe it as like a bad flatmate finally moving out), therapy helped me understand where the voices were coming from in the first place. If this is something you'd like to explore, there are some books listed at the end of the book that might help you.

The meaning of Big and Brave might change for you as time goes on. For example, when I first went to my GP to talk about my mental health, I almost vomited with fear before crossing the threshold. To tell someone how mad I felt was the Biggest and Bravest thing I could do. Now, for me, to be Big and Brave is to believe that I am worth taking care of and that investing time into doing so is worth it too. It means not seeing myself as an ongoing project of a human, needing to be perfected, but as a messy, real-life person, needing to be loved and nurtured.

93

Look after your sexual health.

Respect your body and look after it. Maybe that means getting an STI check, even if you're nervous of what the outcome might be. If you're not sexually active, you still need to look after yourself – schedule in a smear test if you have one due, and get to know what feels normal in your body, e.g. check your breasts or testicles, and talk to your GP if anything changes.

94

Track your time for a
week to see how much
free time you have, and
where you can carve
out moments to focus
on self-care – or to
spend more time doing
an activity you love.

95

Be honest with yourself about your
mental health journey – how often do
you feel overwhelmed? How do you
feel physically when you get panicked?
Is there a family medical history you
should know about? Check in with your
GP if something stands out to you. In
Anxiety for Beginners, Eleanor Morgan
talks about different treatment options,
the physiological process of a panic
attack, and her own personal journey.
It armed me with the information I
needed to go to my GP and ask for what
I needed. You may find other books
more relevant to your experiences –
seek them out to give you the courage
and information you need to get help.

96

My dad always gives me the same advice when I'm stressed or worried about something: select a point on your way home where you'll deposit some of your worries. It can be a certain bus stop, or a tree in the park. You'll leave them there, and pick them up the next morning. This is a twist on a CBT technique called 'parking'. You set aside a point (metaphorical or literal) in your day where you'll leave your worries, giving you space to breathe until you pick them up again.

SEE
YOU LATER,
PAL

(OR
(NEVER)

97

Set a goal for yourself that
is realistic to achieve.

———

Using a bullet journal as a habit
tracker is a great way to do this.[13]
You can see yourself taking steps
towards your goal (like 'run 5k'
or 'keep Monday evenings free to
relax'), rather than putting endless
pressure on yourself to achieve an
amorphous goal (like 'get healthier'
or 'spend more time relaxing'). The
key is to make the journey just as
important as the destination.

98

Make plans for the future. If you're not sure what you would prefer or might feel up to, you can always cancel! Plan to enjoy the future, and wring all the joy you can from anticipating how much fun you will have.

99

Encourage your friends to hold you accountable – not in a fitspo way, but in a 'You asked us to check in, so we're checking in' way.

———

My boyfriend has been amazing at this – recently I did not want to get out of bed for the whole day, and he gently said, 'I know you will feel better if you have a shower and sit on the sofa, so I need you to do that now. I know you don't want to, but I promise it will help.' And it did.

100

Keep a mood diary and share it.

In Emily Reynolds' book *A Beginner's Guide to Losing Your Mind*, she talks about how she uses a mood diary as part of her bipolar self-care regimen. You create a scale for your moods from one to ten, and note down any other info about how you're feeling or external factors that might affect you (e.g. exercise, alcohol). There are plenty of examples of mood diaries online – or if you buy Emily's book (you should! It's good!), there are examples at the back.

101

Be more compassionate towards
yourself, and try not to beat yourself
up over perceived failures. Your
best effort will look different on
different days, but the amount
of effort you're putting in stays
the same. I used to think: *I'll get
better; this isn't the real me.* But it
is you! You are a whole person, no
matter how you may feel. Honest.

Finally, find out what works for you.
I'm loathe to prescribe a fix-all solution
for All Mental Health Problems.
Get out a pen, go back through this
book, and circle or underline anything
you think might help *you*. If you think
the opposite of any of these tips will
help you, then scribble out my words and
write down your own.

NOTES

1.   Arianna Rebolini, 'Getting Rid of Clothes I Hated Helped Me Love My Body', *BuzzFeed*, 21 July 2016. www.buzzfeed.com/ariannarebolini/instead-of-losing-weight-i-just-lost-the-clothes-7vd?utm_term=.gcVxPwB7W#.pgmmooPZJ

2.   Bryony Gordon, *Mad Girl* (Headline, 2016), p294.

3.   If you want to read up on the science, check out this article: Rita Berto, 'Exposure to restorative environments helps restore attentional capacity', *Journal of Environmental Psychology* (Vol. 25, 3), September 2005, pp249–59. www.sciencedirect.com/science/article/pii/S0272494405000381

4.   The Nursery and Garden Industry Australia provides this brief report, based on findings

from the New University of Technology Sydney:
'The Positive Effects of Office Plants', *Nursery
Papers*, (Issue 6), July 2010. www.ngia.com.au/
Story?Action=View&Story_id=1686

5.   The Twitter thread has since been deleted, but
Tandoh quoted her tweet and wrote about the idea
in a piece for *The Pool*: 'There's joy to be found in
everything we eat', 2 February 2018.
www.the-pool.com/food-home/food-honestly/2018/5/
Ruby-Tandoh-on-finding-the-joy-in-all-food

6.   Future Work Centre, 'You've Got Mail!
Research Report 2015', 2015.
www.futureworkcentre.com/wp-content/uploads/2015/07/
FWC-Youve-got-mail-research-report.pdf

7.   Dr Anne-Marie Chang, as told to *Scientific
American*. Jessica Schmerler, 'Q&A: Why Is Blue
Light before Bedtime Bad for Sleep?', 1 September
2015. www.scientificamerican.com/article/q-a-why-is
-blue-light-before-bedtime-bad-for-sleep
   Dr Chang and colleagues' original research
paper: 'Evening use of light-emitting eReaders

negatively affects sleep, circadian timing, and next-morning alertness', *Proceedings of the National Academy of Sciences of the United States of America* 112.4 (2015): 1232–1237, PMC, Web, 1 May 2018.

8.   Beauty Banks provide toiletries to people in the UK who are homeless or on low incomes, via food banks and homeless shelters. They accept boxes of toiletries sent to them directly, or you can donate items online at: www.easho.co.uk/beauty -bank. Read more about the scheme at: www.the-pool.com/beauty/beauty-honestly/2018/7/Sali-Hughes -and-Jo-Jones-launch-Beauty-Banks

9.   Mind's introduction to mental health problems for friends and family (2017): www.mind.org.uk/information-support/types-of-mental-health-problems/mental-health-problems-introduction/for-friends-family

   Rethink's guidance: www.rethink.org/carers-family -friends

10.   Mind has produced Guides to Wellness Action Plans for both employees and employers to

support the mental health of their staff. You can download these for free at: mind.org.uk/workplace/mental-health-at-work/taking-care-of-your-staff/employer-resources/wellness-action-plan-download

11.   Susan Calman, *Cheer Up Love* (Two Roads, 2016).

12.   Gary Chapman's site includes an assessment to find out your preferred way of communicating, or 'love language'. www.5lovelanguages.com

13.   For guidance on starting a bullet journal, you might want to check out this article, which makes it super clear: 'WTF Is A Bullet Journal And Why Should You Start One? An Explainer', *BuzzFeed*, 31 May 2016. www.buzzfeed.com/rachelwmiller/how-to-start-a-bullet-journal?utm_term=.ie4G1BdXd#.ec7x90BQB

READING LIST

These are the handful of books referenced throughout the book. I've tried to choose texts that talk about a variety of mental health issues, written by people from a variety of backgrounds – and most importantly, they're all books that I've read, loved, and read again. You should be able to find them all in your local library.

ANXIETY FOR BEGINNERS by Eleanor Morgan
(Bluebird, 2016)
Eleanor writes about the physiology and neurology of anxiety in a calm and informed way, drawing from her own experiences. This is the book I pass on to anyone who wants to learn more about what it's like living with anxiety day to day.

CHEER UP LOVE by Susan Calman (Two Roads, 2016)
Susan writes about depression, creativity and coming out – as well as chatting through some techniques which have helped her over the years, and some 10/10 jokes.

MAD GIRL by Bryony Gordon (Headline, 2016)
Bryony writes about her OCD and parenting, and manages to be both laugh-out-loud funny at the same time as writing straight from the soul.

A BEGINNER'S GUIDE TO LOSING YOUR MIND by Emily Reynolds (Hodder & Stoughton, 2017)
Emily writes about living with bipolar disorder and how to 'navigate staying sane'. This is an invaluable book for younger readers, as Emily lays out everything you might need to know about dealing with mental health professionals, as well as practical daily tips.

REMEMBER THIS WHEN YOU'RE SAD by Maggy Van Eijk (Lagom, 2018)

Maggy writes about anxiety, depression and borderline personality disorder, and details how getting a diagnosis isn't always a cure. She's sweet and funny and reassuring.

HOW TO GROW STUFF by Alice Vincent (Ebury, 2017)

Alice writes about easy, helpful tips to help anyone grow a garden – no matter what their confidence level is. Although it's a book about gardening, it will give you so much more than that.

ACKNOWLEDGEMENTS

Of all the things I thought I'd write a book about, I never thought it would be about my anxiety. It's thanks to my friends, family and online pals that I did.

Thank you, Chris, for being my sweet otter half. Thanks, Mum, Dad, Rob and Rory, for always encouraging me to be kinder to myself. Thanks, my lovely Scruffs, for always listening. Thanks, Tabatha, Kim, Chelsey, Emma and Tolani, for being the eternal queens of my heart. Thanks, Diane, for getting me this far. Thanks, Juliet, the best agent I could ask for, and Kiera, who steered this book with the gentlest and wisest hand. Thanks, Naoise, for creating my ideal dog in illustrated form. And thanks to everyone who I've quoted in this book – you made me brave enough to write it.